TINA LEVENE

Heartbeat of a R.E.A.L. Leader

Discovering your strengths

while celebrating other's gifts

Tina Levene

TINA LEVENE

Heartbeat of a R.E.A.L. Leader

Cover Designs by Alex Massey

Developmentally Edited & Published in collaboration with RoseDale Inc.
3030 Starkey Blvd, Suite 207
Trinity Florida 34655

www.CraftingYourMessage.com

www.CreatingYourBook.com

Printed in the United States of America, First Edition

ISBN: 987-0-9911200-8-6

HEARTBEAT OF A R.E.A.L. LEADER

TINA LEVENE

Dedication

This book is dedicated to my late Grandmother, Pauline Miller, and my Father, Tim Miller. Thank you for teaching me through your actions, inside and outside of your workplaces, that people matter, deserve respect, and there is hope for every human being. Your leadership skills demonstrated to me more than you could have ever spoken. To both of you and the strong work ethic richly instilled by your example, I credit my professional success as a leader.

TINA LEVENE

Introduction

Sick and tired of being *sick and tired*? Want to feel appreciated and celebrated at work? Overwhelmed with a negative team that is intimidated by your job title? Despair of ever leading a successful team? Don't know how to influence or inspire others? Afraid to step into your leadership position? I have felt every one of these things and more!

For many years, I did not see myself as a leader, but I do now because I have learned a few lessons along the way.

Ready to... achieve your dreams? Accomplish your goals? Build a respectful and productive team? Lead with confidence and mindfulness? Empower your circle of influence? Become a R.E.A.L. leader? Take your team to the next level? This book is written for you!

Ever felt like you hit bottom in your professional life? I have good news for you, there is only one way to look from there- UP! I have learned to be grateful for my unfortunate experiences with damaging leadership. Because of them, I've gained knowledge, education, and experience which has equipped and qualified me to write this book. I'm here to guide you and your team to the next level!

Believe me when I tell you, "I've seen it all!" I've worked in the fields of social work and juvenile justice for decades. I've conducted investigations of incidents of abuse, neglect, and abandonment of children. I've also worked as a Program

Evaluator and Critical Incidents Reporter in facilities which provide care for youth.

I often found leaders who were not equipped to effectively lead, and employees who were burnt out. Both cost employers time, money, and energy! To say the least, "I was sick and tired of being sick and tired!"

It seemed like obstacles were flying at me from every direction. I was overwhelmed by negative colleagues. I experienced sexual harassment, religious discrimination, and emotional neglect at the hands of leadership. I even had to file charges against a client who brought a loaded gun to the school where I worked and threatened to kill me.

So, what did I do? I quit social work after only three years and went to work on a cruise ship! My attempt at a *geographical cure* didn't resolve my issues, and to be honest, I doubt it's the right answer for you.

Eventually, I dove back in. I worked many grant-funded jobs and was required to reestablish myself time and time again due to budget cuts and a lack of job security. I believe I survived the challenges of my employment history for a purpose.

At times, our pain overshadows our passion and distracts us from our purpose. This book was written to help you navigate through the painful times and move toward your passion and purpose.

If I can help one person become a life-changing leader who supports their team and creates a safe environment where their gifts flourish, my purpose has been fulfilled.

There is great value in discovering your strengths in challenging times. We all know the most precious of gems are created under pressure! A R.E.A.L. leader learns to thrive amidst challenges, and never leaves a team member behind.

A R.E.A.L. leader makes personal sacrifices to take care of the ones who make you look good. I am not saying it is not important to take care of yourself; I am saying that when team members feel safe and valued, they will work to their full potential. A R.E.A.L. leader provides acknowledgement, affirmation, and appreciation. R.E.A.L. leaders celebrate other's gifts in challenging times and good times.

The Heartbeat of a R.E.A.L. Leader is about learning to stand strong, becoming an advocate for your team and above all, remaining coachable.

I hope this resonates with you; the world needs more R.E.A.L. leaders. Your unique gifts, talents, and strengths can lead your company, business, church, or school to success! This book has been written to encourage and equip you to keep going.

It will make you smile and laugh out loud at times. You may not fall on the floor unable to get up or laugh a proverbial body part off, but I promise you'll feel uplifted.

It will catapult your professional life to the next level, and enhance your personal life, by equipping you with top-notch tools. The skills presented in this book have proven legendary results. Follow the *It is Time to Get R.E.A.L.* Action Steps provided at the end of each chapter to reveal the secrets which will help you develop the skills to support and grow a successful team.

Ready to experience freedom from self-doubt and negativity? Learn strategies to bridge the gap with co-workers who are not "in it to win it"? Work in harmony with "strangers" who you ultimately spend more time a day with than your own family? Create a safe, positive, and productive work environment?

It is time to get excited about your work and enjoy your role as a leader! It's time to discover the heartbeat of the R.E.A.L. leader *within you*, celebrate others, and experience legendary results!

Table of Contents

Chapter One

Discovering Your Leadership Potential

"To handle yourself, use your head: to handle others, use your heart."

- Eleanor Roosevelt

TINA LEVENE

Chapter One

On a farm in small-town Ohio, Tim, the youngest of three boys, grew up in a basement home with no plumbing. He was a rambunctious boy who struggled to pass classes in school every day of his overly active life. Yet, at a young age, he managed to convert his energy into a dedicated work ethic. He was labeled a 'hard worker' which barely scratched the surface of his desirable traits.

In 1965, at the age of sixteen, Tim eagerly accepted a job at the local grocery store. He could already feel the money earned by his hard work burning a hole in his pocket. He bagged groceries for patrons, returned grocery carts scattered throughout the parking lot to the store, and picked up trash from the ground.

Tim volunteered to fight for our country in the Vietnam War, when he was just eighteen years old, and was whisked off to boot camp before the ink was even dry on his enlistment paperwork. His dedication and work ethic paid off again when his exceptional exercise regimen made him the fittest soldier his new Sergeant had ever encountered. With the successful completion of boot camp, Tim's unit was squeezed into a crowded plane destined for the dangers of war in Vietnam.

Within a few months of deployment, Tim received multiple wounds and lost his sight in one eye, earning a ticket home. The two purple hearts for heroism that arrived by mail were but a silent gesture of gratitude for the price he paid for our freedom in those jungles. War had changed Tim; no longer the same young man who had departed from a small town in Ohio, he refused the free college education. Passing on job opportunities and spiraling into a violent, destructive, alcoholic path, Tim sought something familiar to ground him.

The small grocery store that gave Tim his first job was the answer; he quickly and easily slipped back into his old position, dedicating his loyalty to this family owned business. During his twenty years with that small store, he never imagined a future where he would open and manage a large warehouse store, but he did.

For twenty-six years, Tim successfully led more than one hundred and sixty employees. His leadership reflected his strong work ethic and personal accomplishment of restoring relationships through his recovery from alcoholism.

Why do I share the story of this man with you? Because, Tim is my Father, and a true testament to having the heartbeat of a R.E.A.L. leader! A revolutionary leader who elevated his team and activated their talents for legendary results.

Revolutionary leaders

Elevate their team and

Activate their talents for

Legendary results

The day before my father retired from his forty-six years in the grocery business, I made time for a visit to the huge warehouse store. It was a chilly winter day in Ohio, but I wanted to personally witness the loyalty and leadership that had made it so great. I was surprised to find my sixty-five-year-old father trudging through the cold and treacherous parking lot to retrieve and return grocery carts to the store.

This unselfish act of kindness was for his teenage employees who were learning by his example, those leaders in training who had great potential but needed direction. Moments later he was picking up trash from the ground, between shaking hands with patrons, and humbly accepting the well wishes for a happy retirement. I had witnessed the reason for his success as a leader.

As a young man, my father did not consider himself a leader. In boot camp his Sergeant had asked him if he was a leader and he replied that he was not. After forty-six years of committed service to a company that barely paid the bills but consumed 60 hours a week of his time, he probably still did not consider himself a leader. But let me tell you what a friend of mine shared with me twenty years AFTER working for my father as a teenager.

"Your father taught me what it was like to be a true leader and a respectful man. I will never forget watching him pick up trash from those nasty floors and thinking, *he's the boss, what is he doing?* His actions always conveyed his huge heart and gentle soul."

You might not identify as a leader right now, but I hope by the end of this book you will discover your strengths and understand the leadership value you bring to your family, job, and community.

> *The discovery of your leadership potential is an ongoing process throughout your life.*

The discovery of your leadership potential is an ongoing process throughout your life. One minute you are just eighteen and wanting to vote; the next minute you are running for President. This is a drastic example, or is it? Both actions risk something and gain something, only you can discover and determine the journey to leadership in your life.

Leaders are not born, they are created, and that creation begins within you. It is how you treat others when no one is watching. It is in humbling yourself to create a level playing field and doing whatever it takes without demeaning your values or the other person. Leadership is the ACTIONS taken by ordinary people that enhance the lives of those around them.

Just as my father doubted his own ability to be a leader, you may question the likelihood of establishing yourself as a leader, or that you even have the characteristics and strengths needed to become a leader. It is my hope that this book will take you on a journey of self-discovery that will lead you to embrace and implement leadership skills.

First and foremost, the roadmap to leadership begins with a self-discovery process. It is a matter of mindset; you must believe you possess the ability to establish leadership qualities OR obtain them. Have you ever heard the saying *fake it 'til you make it?* While I do not believe in faking anything, the saying speaks to the idea that your mindset has a powerful influence over your outcomes.

> *Leadership is the ACTIONS taken by ordinary people that enhance the lives of those around them.*

Leadership requires a willingness to stand firm and fulfill the responsibilities necessary while accepting the role and title. Your thoughts will steer your life in a positive or negative direction; where your mind goes, your body will soon follow. The choice is ultimately yours.

Laughter is a great example of this concept. Think about a time when you had been frustrated or having a bad moment at work, then a co-worker said or did something to make you laugh. Did you notice how your frustration swiftly dissipated like the cloud of hanging seeds blown from a dandelion flower?

POOF... and your frustration is gone. Your negative thoughts vanished by replacing them with positive ones. Consider how this process could transform your hours, days, weeks, months, or your life!

Your attitudes determine your energy, motivation, and capabilities to achieve great tasks. I have an example of this for you. After smoking for many years, I was sharing a smoke break with my supervisor, Carol, and rambling on about how sick and tired I was of smoking.

I smelled, it was gross, and I hated having to schedule my breaks around my need to smoke. My hatred toward the addiction that had its deathly grip on me was finally getting to be too much.

I will never forget what she said to me that day. Carol, being a licensed counselor herself, turned to me and said, "Tina, you are so stubborn, you will probably quit smoking and never pick it up again!"

For the first time, I looked at what I considered to be a negative characteristic, a character defect or annoying personality trait, and realized I could flip that stubbornness to use it for something positive!

In 2001, I finally got sick and tired of being sick and tired... and I used my stubbornness to quit smoking. Proof positive that our mind and personality characteristics can be a wellspring of untapped potential for us.

It is time to get R.E.A.L.

Envision your true potential and really believe that you have the ability to reach that potential. There is great power in self-belief; it can make you or break you. Not one other person is exactly like you, with your strengths and challenges, and not one other person will lead like you do.

Try these Action Steps:

List your strengths, those abilities that make you unique.

Then list your challenges, those limitations that keep you from your potential.

Do you need to work on your communication skills?

Do you have a hard time visualizing the solution to a problem?

This self-evaluation will help you determine your positives and negatives.

Often, people will judge themselves harshly one way or another; completely positive or totally negative. Either way, you are misrepresenting yourself and your potential.

Practice the skill of turning negative character defects into positives.

Try these Action Steps:

On a scale of 0 (not a leader) to a 10 (a real leader), how would you rate your leadership skills?

How far are you from a 10 on that scale, and what do you need to do to reach it?

Which character defects could you transform into positive attributes to increase your leadership skills?

Have a trusted colleague rate you on that same scale and see if you see yourself the same way as they do and if not, why?

Your journey of self-discovery to your leadership potential is underway; enjoy the process.

"Those that criticize you, don't have time to build themselves up because they waste their time, money and energy. Just like that time I rented a DVD and forgot to watch it!"

\-   *Tina Levene*

TINA LEVENE

Chapter Two

Identifying Your Leadership Vision

"If your actions inspire others to dream more, learn more, do more and become more, you are a leader."

- *John Quincy Adams*

TINA LEVENE

Remember my supervisor, Carol, she was one of my favorites. She had many of the characteristics of a phenomenal boss, was an exceptional leader and a well-respected colleague in the community. Great leaders like her are responsible and have laser focus on the mission at hand.

Do you have a favorite supervisor, maybe an awesome boss you really admire? How about a CEO you really enjoy spending time with at work or even outside of work? Are you thinking of that person right now? Keep them in mind as we venture into a vision for you and your leadership journey.

Imagine that boss or supervisor and their many admirable characteristics. What was their personality like at work? Are there any traits you wish you had as well? What type of positive attributes did they contribute to the team? Perhaps their job title was not that of supervisor or boss, but maybe their leadership skills overshadowed their occupational position in the company.

During one of my training breakout sessions I asked, *"What are the characteristics of your favorite boss?"* My audience of child caregivers, social workers, after school program supervisors and youth program providers filled up three flip chart pages with descriptive words! Many of those characteristics would probably describe your favorite boss, too. I believe those qualities create a true leader, an exceptional supervisor, and an awesome boss.

The most common feedback I receive indicates the leaders we admire most provide a sense of SAFETY. Why would that be true? Feelings of safety are key to successful family life and personal or professional friendships; we all perform at our best when we feel safe. A leader that develops and fosters a safe environment will gain the trust of their team. This will increase production and encourage effective communication for networking at its best. The SAFE supervisor communicates effectively and appropriately with subordinates.

On occasion, I have observed some leaders being aggressive and demanding when communicating with staff members. Keep in mind that a large part of communication is non-verbal in nature, such as gestures, facial expressions, and body language. Creating a feeling of safety is a fundamental key in developing leaders who can visualize the potential of the mission at hand.

Participating in Yoga class has taught me the importance of balance. What is stretched on one side of the body must be stretched on the other side of the body as well or it will create an imbalance. The opposite of a safe and professional atmosphere is that of a hostile or threatening workplace.

My goal here is not to create a blame game or slam session, merely to identify the need to foster a safe environment and point out the potential for harmful or negative behaviors. Stay with me here as we STRETCH both sides of this important topic.

Unfortunately, one of my past work experiences developed into a threatening and hostile work environment for me and my co-workers. The names and locations will not be disclosed to protect the guilty, but the danger consumed a well-known, billion-dollar, International Agency. When an agency almost crumbles at the feet of ONE employee who caused that much chaos, the value of safety becomes evident.

If as a leader you do not make workplace safety a priority, you risk the very foundation of the company.

Leaders can develop a safe work environment by embracing a few simple qualities: a healthy work ethic, a positive proactive attitude, integrity, and simply being a caring person. Healthy work ethic can be learned over time on the job, BUT a strong work ethic ingrained in the family DNA is truly a gift.

The summer I was nine years old, my Grandmother took me to work with her at the local elementary school. She paid me a few cents to help her as she made copies of the student handbook, assembled the 20 pages and stapled them together. As you can imagine, it was time consuming to make all those copies, pile up hundreds of pages and compile each book by hand for the students.

At a very young age, my Grandmother was teaching me the importance of organization, consideration of space, and most importantly the value of a safe environment while developing healthy work ethics that were both appropriate and balanced. Any time I might whine about a paper cut or that a page did not copy correctly, my Grandmother would tell me, "Do not waste your time complaining!" She taught me to use my energy for moving forward in life. "Go ahead, keep moving Tina!" were the last words she spoke to me before losing her power of speech to Alzheimer's.

R.E.A.L. leaders believe their team members can be trained up to become leaders at some point.

Later in life when we walked together she would motion in front of her wheelchair for me to keep walking and not stop to wait for her. As a natural born leader and women's Army Corps Veteran during World War II, it must have been a challenge for her to allow others to walk in front of her… or was it?

Exceptional leaders believe in their team AND their own ability to lead them. My Grandmother taught me to do for myself. She endorsed an independent lifestyle that would pave the way for me to become a leader. R.E.A.L. leaders believe their team members can be trained up to become leaders at some point.

You might believe that leaders should always be in the forefront but that will never allow others to grow into leaders. I believe a team that feels safe, supported and understood will succeed where a team that feels threatened, undermined and misunderstood, cannot. Have you experienced that negative environment before? It is not conducive to a healthy, positive, and safe workplace!

April 21, 2017, Psychology Today published an article by Dr. Gretchen Watson that is note-worthy.

> "Three Ways to Boost Workplace Safety"
>
> "Safety training is important, but it's only as effective as the employees are engaged - are willing to go the extra mile, take personal ownership for the quality of their work, and are proud of their jobs. Highly engaged employees are more likely to take error prevention practices seriously and improving employee engagement is often the most effective way to ensure processes don't set people up for failure. This is true whether you are trying to avoid physical injuries or other costly errors."
>
> "Three ways to improve employee engagement are to:
>
> - Let employees know their contribution is meaningful

- Recognize people for a job well done
- Treat everyone with dignity and respect

Safety isn't just about providing training. It involves keeping employees happy, healthy, and motivated. No matter how safety is defined in your organization, it cannot be achieved unless employees are committed and involved."

Let's be real, I am not saying we should expect leaders to be perfect. No one is perfect. For those that think they are perfect, I know it is hard to be humble when you are great. Try to remember that we are all just a work in progress, moving us and our mission forward.

The development of leadership qualities can be likened to the ripening process of fruit. If you pick the fruit too soon (rush someone into leadership) it is hard, tasteless or bitter and NOT enjoyable. It may even discourage you from trying that fruit again.

If you wait patiently (patience, guidance and understanding), add some sunlight (positive energy) and water (thirst for knowledge), then at the appropriate time you can harvest the ripe fruit. That delicious, tender fruit will bring enjoyment and satisfaction.

Picture a fresh peach as you bite into it and the juices run down your arm, yum! What happens if you leave the fruit too long, forget about it or do not nurture it (or it's potential); it will rot. The fruit becomes nasty; it is discolored, smells bad, and falls apart. Some fruit (and people) will even turn slimy!

My hope is for this book to assist you in identifying a vision for yourself as a leader. Remember the saying, *fake it 'til you make it*, this is your opportunity to *envision it before you become it*!

Your team members want to feel valued and included. When you value their gifts and talents it makes delegating duties easy. I cover talents in another chapter, but I wanted to introduce it here first to encourage you to start to think of how you can delegate duties to help you manage your time and better organize your priorities.

A positive, proactive approach to leadership will help you utilize your employee's gifts and work together to accomplish more. Now that you have an idea of some of the characteristics of your favorite boss,

> *Remember the saying fake it 'til you make it, this is your opportunity to envision it before you become it!*

I have a big question for you! Are you the kind of leader that you would want to follow?

It is time to get R.E.A.L.

A revolutionary leader is:

- Coachable

- Willing to learn

- Always willing to take time to understand others.

Your attitude should embody 100% respect toward your team members. This leadership journey begins with you, your willingness to identify your leadership potential, and all the expectations of your performance.

One of my favorite quotes is, "Stop pointing your finger at others when you have four fingers point back at you!" If you point out the faults or mistakes of others, you have four fingers pointing back at you.

Try These Actions Steps:

Examine yourself and make a list

- Examine your strengths

- Examine your weaknesses

After you have done that remember, as a leader you must always examine yourselves, your motives, your strengths, and your weaknesses before blaming a team member for a circumstance at work.

Determine what you can do to enhance your strengths and mitigate your weaknesses. It is better to focus on making your strengths stronger and finding other ways and other people to compensate for your weaknesses.

Focus on your progress as a leader, not on perfection. Keep moving forward; do not waste your time or energy whining. Build your credibility by having integrity inside and outside of the workplace.

Be your favorite boss! Be the kind of leader that you would follow.

Most importantly, be your best version of you!

"Be YOU, everyone else is taken. And whatever you do, always treat yourself like your own best friend! Or treat me like your own best friend, my address is..."

- *Tina Levene*

TINA LEVENE

Chapter Three

Accepting Your Leadership Position

"Only changed people can change the world."

-   *Rick Warren*

TINA LEVENE

Chapter Three

We started this journey of discovery talking about your leadership potential and how your strengths and abilities are an important part of becoming a R.E.A.L. Leader.

Our next step was identifying your vision of leadership by listing the characteristics of your favorite boss or supervisor. This generated descriptive labels, like coachable, ethical, and responsible, that you can use on your path to leadership.

Now let's determine where you fit in and how you can empower your team, so they feel like they belong. To create a *masterpiece*, every team member needs to buy into the common mission and goals, so they will follow their leader. This book, *Heartbeat of a R.E.A.L. Leader,* is about the truth of HOW a great leader really leads.

First and foremost, you belong here! During my keynote presentations and breakout sessions on leadership, I hand each participant a puzzle piece. It is an actual piece of a puzzle that I purchase before the event, based on the number expected in attendance. Usually, I allow each person to choose the piece they want and then all together we hold up our pieces and repeat after me, "I belong here. I am valuable. I am essential to this masterpiece. I am not a mistake. I am needed."

This exercise is a reminder that we are each a piece of something much larger than ourselves. Believe it or not, many people do not feel like they are a part of the team.

> *The truth is, a sense of belonging and safety are factors that work in harmony for the creation of your masterpiece.*

My most popular keynote topic and bestselling workbook for professionals is *Preventing Burn-Out, Igniting Passion!* It shares how over half of all employees are burnt out in their current position and over seventy percent are dreaming of a different position or job.

If you really think about those statistics, you can see that not many people really enjoy their current employment. They are burnt out, overwhelmed, frustrated, and not happy. Full of all that negativity, they probably feel like they are disconnected from their team, they are not able to contribute to the company vision, and that they just don't belong.

A need to belong or be a part of something is innate in every human being. Look at how much time we spend participating in clubs, extracurricular activities, sororities, fraternities, social elite clubs, political parties, teams, classes, and religious groups. They give us a sense of belonging to something; you might say we are pack beings! These examples meet a need in us but also emphasize the need for great leadership. If a leader is not established, total chaos erupts.

We discussed earlier how important it was to create a safe environment for your team. Imagine if each of your team members felt like they belonged AND felt safe at your place of employment. When a person feels protected and safe from negativity, their performance improves, they show up on time each day, and they are more likely to avoid burn-out. The truth is, a sense of belonging and safety are factors that work in harmony for the creation of your masterpiece.

So, what is the masterpiece? This is the vision you have for your company, agency, school or church that you invite your team to assist you in accomplishing! Together you must create a comprehensive plan for your masterpiece that will include how each player will contribute to the journey. I suggest a brainstorming session with a storyboard or creative work group to determine the look, feel, and outcome of the masterpiece. Be sure to give everyone a voice and allow team members to utilize their gifts. Be creative!

Remember the puzzle pieces? If you look at a puzzle piece you will notice that one side has the printed picture on it and the other is blank. The printed

> *Your gifts, talents and abilities are what brought you to your job and position in this moment.*

side symbolizes your past, your history, the part of your life you cannot change. The blank side is your right now, your future, your ability to create your life from this point forward. Which side is more important or powerful?

The printed side is important because it represents those lessons you encountered that developed you into the person you are today and shaped your character. The printed side is what positions you in the masterpiece. Your gifts, talents and abilities are what brought you to your job and position in this moment. The printed side cannot be changed; it is your history. Done. Finished. Now, place your printed side into the masterpiece. See, you belong. Without you, the masterpiece would be incomplete - unfinished.

The blank side is equally important, it represents hope for the future, and exhilarating opportunities to succeed. You cannot see what is yet to come; the unknown sparks curiosity, and an eagerness to experience it that results in ambition to move forward. While these emotions are exciting for many, they can be overwhelming to a person uninterested in wandering out of their comfort zone.

Fear of the unknown can feel like a free-fall into questionable circumstances that will ultimately result in failure and disappointment. Morbid sounding but true, the only concrete reality for our future is that we will all die someday. Take a chance, step into the unknown; you are worth the risk

I have enjoyed living in sunny Clearwater, Florida with my husband and son since 2009. Before then, we lived in Ohio, but vacationed here for years. I wanted to do more than visit so every time we visited, I covertly applied for jobs. My husband had no idea!

In early January 2009, we were driving back to Ohio through freezing rain on the icy mountain roads of West Virginia. As he carefully navigated the treacherous terrain, my frustration grew until I couldn't stand it a moment longer and yelled, "Why can't we just move to Florida?"

He was surprised, but quickly rambled off three important reasons we could not move to paradise. "Honey, you know I love my job teaching dance to inner city youth. And we just bought our dream home less than two years ago. We can't forget Saint. He already runs away back to the old house. Imagine what that dog would do if we moved all the way to Florida."

After an exhausting drive, we arrived safely at our dream home in Ohio. Sadly, I thought to myself, *we are not in paradise. This is anything but sunny blue skies, white powdery sand, and aqua ocean waves.*

We were surrounded by an ocean of Midwest winter greys, but some unexpected events took place that January. First, I received a phone call for a job interview, and that interview led to a job offer. Then, our six-year-old dog unexpectedly died. And my husband lost his job, which led to the loss of our dream home.

The moral of the story is coming, stay with me, folks. When the universe wants you to shift directions, it begins with a desire, and often unexpected events happen that lead to change. Fortunately, for my family, our path was re-directed to paradise – Clearwater, Florida. Because, yes, I accepted the job offer and we moved to Florida. Somedays I still pinch myself to be sure we really live near one of the most beautiful beaches in the United States.

We lived in an apartment near the nine-mile bridge across Tampa Bay. Day after day, as I commuted over the bridge into Tampa traffic, I drew serenity from the breathtaking view. At the last traffic light, before hitting the traffic of the busy city, there is an outdoor area with picnic tables and BBQ pits where families and friends can relax and enjoy the beautiful scenery.

One morning as I sat at the light, I noticed a van parked in the handicapped spot with its back doors open and a ramp extending from the vehicle. Nearby, was a woman painting a blank canvas on an easel while her husband watched, motionless, from his wheelchair.

She seemed like an angel as each brush stroke captured the beauty of nature and paradise. I imagined her masterpiece of lively, dancing colors brought hope to the tired eyes of her husband as he observed. Just like our puzzle pieces, there are two sides to this story. The blank canvas, awaiting the creative use of our gifts, is like the blank side of the puzzle piece. Observing the creation of the masterpiece, is like fitting the printed pieces together.

> *Your mission as a leader is to create a safe environment for your team, where they feel valuable.*

Whether you are creating on the blank side, or fitting the printed side together, accepting your leadership position requires recognizing the value of both sides of each puzzle piece. Choose to utilize the gifts of your team members and create the motivation and enthusiasm to accomplish a masterpiece together. One day, you may be the painter; the next day, you may be an observer of greatness.

Your mission as a leader is to create a safe environment for your team, where they feel valuable. There they will accomplish great things and perform the tasks necessary to complete the masterpiece, the vision laid out before you. Each person's gifts and abilities will contribute to the masterpiece. Stand firmly in your leadership role, understanding that every employee is priceless. Team members will come and go over time. Regardless of how they fit in, you the leader, are responsible for bringing all the pieces masterfully together.

It is time to get R.E.A.L.

A R.E.A.L. leader values both the printed and the blank side of each piece of the puzzle and skillfully fits each piece into its place in the masterpiece. Each team member's uniqueness is highlighted which creates a culture of tribal approval. When you know that you are valued, you fit, you belong, fears for the future are minimized and a sense of the coming good is increased.

In the grand scheme of life, past, present and future, accepting and standing firm in your leadership position is monumental in bringing the pieces together for your team and for you, both personally and professionally.

Try these Action Steps:

- Assess how your team fits together and the roles or duties of each team member.

- Look at each team member to determine their areas of strength.

- Ask if they are in the correct position in the company or on the team.

- Decide if they can be moved or given different tasks, so they can work from a position of strength.

"With some people, you may need to dig deeper to find their treasures. Others offer it openly on the surface; just below the giant X."

- *Tina Levene*

TINA LEVENE

Chapter Four

Defining Your Leadership Purpose

*"Leaders don't force people to follow,
they invite them on a journey."*

- Charles Lauer

TINA LEVENE

.

Although I don't want to sound overly spiritual in this leadership book, I do feel compelled to share a truth with you as we start this next part of your leadership journey.

YOU were born on purpose and for a purpose. Seriously, you were created for a purpose. That purpose might be to clean the toilets in your local fast food restaurant or it might be leading a million-dollar corporation. Your position and progress will vary depending on your passion to accomplish your personal or professional goals.

Think of purpose as the backbone of your plan, giving you clarity to succeed. Each step along the way is a small milestone that moves you to the next level and ultimately to accomplishing the big victory.

Why do we need to have steps of progression to accomplish our plan or purpose?

Imagine if you will, the game of baseball BUT second base has been removed. You have a runner on first base who waits eagerly for the opportunity to advance and put a run on the board. The All-Star batter steps up to the plate and, BAM, smacks one out of the park for a home run. As he is jogging toward first base he sees the previous runner still occupies the base with a confused look on his face and hands raised in question, with no idea where to proceed. Second base is a step in the progression of the game.

> *The face of a leader is Fearless, Focused, and Forward Thinking.*

There is a rhyme and reason to the rules, regulations, plans, procedures and steps of the game AND in leadership. This chapter will look at your place and purpose in leadership and assist you in recognizing the *face of a leader*.

What does a leader look like? What qualities do you expect to find in a leader? In other words, what does the *face of a leader* look like to you? For me the face of a leader is Fearless, Focused and Forward Thinking. Ideally in that order but achieving them all is an incredible accomplishment. Remember, the expectation is not that the leader is perfect. We are focusing on progress rather than perfection.

Your initial response to being fearless may be the visual of a superhero, cascading off high buildings to fight evil villains, fire and lightning bolts piercing the night sky as the hero rescues victims of crime and returns them home, safe and sound. If so, you might be a comic book fan or a superhero in training!

Being a leader does not require death defying feats of heroism or rescuing anyone. It is really quite simple, so just sit back and relax while we journey into "The Face of a Leader: 101."

Being Fearless is a state of mind. While it can't be purchased or drilled into someone, it can be developed over time, learned bit by bit and practiced often both personally and professionally. Many historical leaders demonstrated this quality.

I can think of a few Presidents, military leaders, and individuals in ministry that appear to be just doing the right thing at the right time, giving no thought to the amount of fear surrounding their decisions or actions. Becoming Fearless is the result of Preparation, Proactivity and Positioning.

Preparation is essential for any leader. Research needs to be done, as well as diving deeper into the subject matter at hand. This stage requires preparing and organizing all data, paperwork and any relevant evidence; not just physical resources but having emotional organization as well.

Emotionally preparing one's mind is just as important as compiling data, especially for the face to face conversations.

> *Becoming Fearless is the result of Preparation, Proactivity, and Positioning.*

Emotional preparation for leaders means developing an action plan in case of angry outbursts, frustrated feelings or just accepting that an escape plan can be initiated if someone's emotions create an uncontrollable situation. Time and energy spent in preparation will ultimately save you time, energy, and money as a Fearless Leader.

Proactivity is the bridge between the preparation and the positioning. Trainings are required to resolve conflicts, to communicate needs and expectations to the team, and to execute the mission or task at hand. Too often, I see leaders who believe they are just reactors. They are forced to put out fires, offer damage control or fix mistakes, when it would be more productive to focus their energy on preparation efforts and being proactive.

Positioning yourself with a fearless attitude conveys a sense of confidence and vision that others may not have. Some leaders may focus on what others are feeling, what the data results say or be too indecisive to get started.

To be Fearless you must feel secure in the plan, be prepared, as well as confident in your position, and in your ability to be proactive in any situation. A clear understanding of the entire process and plan is an absolute must if you are going to be Fearless.

When I think of a Fearless leader, I automatically think of Fire Fighters. They risk their lives each and every day, by running toward danger while others are running away BUT the majority of their job is training, preparing for danger, and being proactive. You might think Fire Fighters are only reactors who extinguish fires but in truth they are the ultimate example of proactivity.

They complete hours of fire-fighting and rescue training, spend time educating children and the community on fire prevention and conducting countless fire drills. Most companies conduct two fires drills each year, making it clear that preparation is the key to preventing fires and causalities from fires.

First and foremost, Fire Fighters are trained to save people from fires and/or accidents, including their own team members. I asked my friend and retired Fire Fighter of forty-five years about the term MAYDAY; he explained that when a fellow Fire Fighter, their brother or sister, is in trouble or trapped in a burning building the team goes in to rescue them. Their motto is, "Leave no man or woman behind," so the team bands together to save or recover them.

Can you imagine if we could create that kind of motto in our offices? Our teams would feel united and protected. We ARE in this together, all accounted for, a team, a work family.

> *When a leader is focused, they are mindful of where they are while always looking forward to the next steps necessary for success.*

Part of a clear understanding is being FOCUSED on the vision and the end results, while not losing sight of the team or their efforts AND being proactive in the process. Distractions happen to the best of us but can become excuses for a lack of success. Adequate preparation, proactive activities and being confident in your positioning is essential to avoiding the pitfalls of distractions.

Have you ever watched a horse race? Did you notice that the horses wear blinkers or blinders? These are small pieces of leather or plastic that attach to the bridle at the side of the horse's head. They reduce the risk of the horse being spooked and minimize distractions in their peripheral vision. In other words, it keeps them focused on the task at hand.

As a leader, we must learn to do the same; stay focused when there is office gossip, incomplete deadlines or when our personal lives spill over to our work life. When a leader is focused, they are mindful of where they are while always looking forward to the next steps necessary for success. Keeping that next step in mind, or forward thinking, will move you toward your goals.

Imagine sitting in your car and looking at your gear shift. P is for park, R is for reverse, N is for neutral, and D is for drive. While you are in park, you are remaining still. Sometimes people remain still out of a fear of failure. After all you don't risk failing if you don't even try.

FAIL is another way of saying - *First Attempt In Learning.*
Everyone has failed, everyone! So long as we learn from that first
attempt, our chances of succeeding are greater than just sitting in
park.

R is for reverse. Who wants to stay in the past? Reverse has only
one function, to move backward. I prefer looking out the front
window of a car because the windshield is so much bigger than
the tiny rear-view mirror. There's a reason for that, you know.

It is important to look at
our past, our history,
what's behind us but not
focus on it too long,
because it begins to
distract us.

> *Forward Thinkers communicate with clarity and purpose, taking 100% responsibility for their attitude and actions.*

The windshield is much bigger, so we can see what's in front of
us, what's in store, so we can prepare, be proactive in our
decisions and position ourselves for safety. We can learn from
our history but then we must move forward.

N or neutral has one use as well. It is only good for determining
or contemplating direction. Have you ever hit the gas only to
realize you are in neutral and not going anywhere? To move you
must choose a direction and change gears!

D or Drive is another term for moving forward. Forward thinking
will "drive" your mission, your company, your organization, and
your attitude. Forward Thinkers communicate with clarity and
purpose, taking 100% responsibility for their attitude and actions.
It encourages consistent peak performance of team members by
inspiring them.

It is time to get R.E.A.L.

Are you getting excited about this leadership journey? Now that you know the three F's of leadership (Fearless, Focused and Forward Thinking) and have a clear understanding of the *face of a leader*, I encourage you to implement these techniques right away. Start small and remain coachable!

Try these Action Steps:

- Attend some trainings to sharpen your skills.

- Learn to dismiss distractions in the office.

- Find ways to create a positive outlook by planning and preparing proactively in the workplace.

Leaders demand excellence in themselves and their teams AND you are now equipped to put on the face of a leader.

Every successful leader builds on their strengths so that their weaknesses become irrelevant. Work on what YOU are good at and become Fearless, Focused, and Forward Thinking!

> *"Even a dull knife can cut through something, but a sharpened knife saves on the cleanup time! I'm referring to pumpkins, people!"*
>
> *- Tina Levene*

TINA LEVENE

Chapter Five

Actions to Becoming a Leader

"What you get by achieving your goals is not as important as what you become by achieving your goals."

-   *Henry David Thoreau*

TINA LEVENE

Chapter Five

During movie production, what is the one word that is yelled right before the clapstick slams down on the clapperboard and the actors begin a new scene? What speaks louder than words? ACTION! Actions will always scream louder than words.

Let's talk about the role of a leader. It is not just a job position or title; it is the role with the greatest responsibility. The actions and words of a leader reflect their overall character AND reflect on the organization, both the negative and the positive.

Leaders never stop learning. Being coachable, with a desire to be trained, is the ultimate attribute of an outstanding leader. It shows a willingness to admit that there is always more to learn. I have never heard a wealthy leader claim, "I know it all, and have done it all, so I can just float through life now and stop learning."

Great leaders understand the value of continued learning and are always open to growing. While goals are important, if you want to leave a legacy you must sharpen your character, mold yourself into a sincere leader, and become more than just a job title.

Another essential aspect of leadership is taking inventory of, and managing, your time and energy. Many of our most influential leaders dress in similar attire every day. *Why would they do that*, you might ask. It uses less of their precious time and energy.

> ***Being coachable, with a desire to be trained, is the ultimate attribute of an outstanding leader.***

They have discovered that the TIME used to shop for different outfits, try them on for fit, and decide which outfit to wear each day, is better used in other ways.

World changers make everyday life as simple as possible, to preserve every ounce of their energy and to focus every second on their mission at hand.

I met a woman recently who does this; she wears the same brands and styles of blouse and skirt each day, but she varies the colors for a different look. She shared with me that it ensures she feels confident and secure both at home and the office.

Another great example of time and energy management is the long-distance swimmer who swam through shark and jellyfish-infested, rough ocean waters from Cuba to Key West, and all without a protective cage. She did not waste energy on the painful, raw, jelly fish stings all over her face and body. She did not waste time doubting her years of strenuous training and preparations for her fifth attempt at this great feat.

When interviewed about her unbelievable and exhausting accomplishment, sixty-four-year old Diana Nyad shared that she trained every day to the same songs, in the same order playing in her head. She memorized the lineup for energy and time management. While swimming one hundred and three miles from Cube to Key West, Diana could tell exactly how far she had come by the song she was singing in her head.

Talk about focus! Her focus was on the mission at hand, swimming from point A to point B as she focused on the music in

> *A leader who focuses on solutions and positivity makes a world of difference in the hustle and bustle of professional life.*

her head. Word after word, song after song, she continued through the pain and pressures to finally accomplish a world record-breaking swim.

Leaders can focus on the problems or the solutions; it is ultimately their choice. Phenomenal communication with their team will alert them to problems, but they need to focus their time and energy on the solutions.

As I mentioned previously, it is important to remain coachable and willing to learn, especially in a solution-focused leadership culture. When leaders focus precious time and energy on positive solutions, it meets the needs of the team members, creating a supportive environment and security in their job positions.

During the busy and mundane duties of the work week, there is value in lifting someone up through encouraging words. Greater yet is the power of positive self-development, which is the equipping of your team with self-care and wellness techniques, that creates a more positive environment and increases productivity.

A leader who focuses on solutions and positivity makes a world of difference in the hustle and bustle of professional life. It is the responsibility of the leader to demonstrate this as an example to their team. Our goal here is to transform and/or fine-tune your leadership skills to not just achieve your goals, but to focus on what you become to your team along the journey.

The list of the responsibilities of a leader could take up every page of this book; the list is never ending really. First and foremost, it goes back to the MAYDAY example and the Fire Fighters motto, "Leave no man or woman behind."

The leader's responsibilities consist of the everyday duties of their position plus the management of a team and the successful completion of THEIR job duties. Overseeing multiple human beings is a huge task and not for the faint of heart. Some of us might even prefer swimming that one hundred and three miles over managing multiple people, who may just show up to collect a pay check.

Leaders are Fearless, Focused, Forward Thinkers who also have great responsibilities; what an exhausting but rewarding job! What if I told you that providing a safe environment was not the ONLY key to establishing a genuine leadership culture? What if I told you that true leaders create more true leaders? Well, it IS true.

Often when asked about leadership, people automatically think it only requires power and control - power of the company, organization or business and control over the employees and job tasks. NOT True, at least in my experiences working with influential leaders from a variety of backgrounds. From PhD's to GED's and billionaires to homeless, the most successful leaders are the ones building up other leaders!

Think back for a minute, previously we identified your vision of leadership by recalling a favorite boss or supervisor. Think about that individual right now and let me ask you a question. Did they mentor, guide and help others to learn how to complete their jobs? I am betting they did. True leaders create more leaders. One of the most important responsibilities of a leader is to train up other leaders.

No one lives forever, so to sustain one's success they must teach others to demonstrate it. Let me give you an example, Zig Ziglar. I remember watching his VHS tapes in the 1990's; I had borrowed from the library to learn the art of sales, and his teaching style mesmerized me! He displayed knowledge, added animation through his storytelling, and offered easy strategies to sell anything. He was a successful leader in the field of sales, but he also really pioneered and demonstrated the concept of leaders creating leaders.

Leaders help others become leaders by running toward danger as a problem solver and conflict resolver! A resolver of conflicts is usually not in a job title or description you would see in an advertisement; however, every successful CEO, COO or CFO is a master at resolving conflicts within the company, both personal and professional. They take care of their team members by resolving conflicts in non-disruptive ways.

> *When a leader takes care of their team, it is a win-win for everyone.*

The role of leadership encompasses the attributes of the Fire Fighter, Diana Nyad and Zig Ziglar examples; all of them spent numerous hours training to become proactive and be prepared for their missions. They share a mindset that teaches others to lead by example, demonstrating effective management skills as well as conflict resolution techniques. When a leader takes care of their team, it is a win-win for everyone.

It is time to get R.E.A.L.

Take care of those in charge of assisting you with your accomplishments and successes.

Now is the time to allow actions to speak louder than words. By your example, not just your job title, you can demonstrate the role of a true leader. Always be coachable and willing to learn more; focus on solutions and positive development for your team, and you will be a true leader.

Most importantly, your greatest responsibility (if you hear nothing else I have said) is to lead others to lead leaders. You are on a mission to create more leaders in your company, business or organization. Take care of those in charge of assisting you with your accomplishments and successes.

Try these Action Steps:

- Identify issues in your environment and make a list of possible solutions.

- Bring your team together and ask them to make their own lists and compare.

- From those ideas, choose at least 2-3 to implement sooner rather than later.

- Work on the other ideas once you get the first 2-3 in place and working.

- Don't be afraid to put some of your team members in charge of the changes and see how they do with you by their side to support them. But give them a chance to LEAD.

"It's time to get R.E.A.L., learn more, complain less and lead others!"

- Tina Levene

TINA LEVENE

Chapter Six

Building a Leadership Team

*"Leaders who don't listen will eventually
be surrounded by people who have
nothing to say."*

- Andy Stanley

TINA LEVENE

Chapter Six

Now that we have defined the role of a leader, we can turn our focus to the team. Building leaders is a significant part of the leadership role. If you are just starting a new position in a company, you might be building a team from the ground up and you will discover the leaders as you build. Maybe you are inheriting a team that you will need to develop into leaders.

How do we find team members who fit our culture and will become great leaders? For current teams, part of the process is identifying the healthy and toxic elements (or strengths and weaknesses) of your growing team. If you are building a new team, the process really starts with advertising, interviewing, hiring, and then nurturing professional relationships with new employees.

First and foremost, we need to start at the beginning: how to advertise for a potential leader. The advertisement verbiage is as important as the actual interview process.

Of course, the ad will include the description of the duties for the position but should also address any pet peeves or expectations you might have for the applicant as a potential leader. For instance, if time management is highly valued you may want to include: *Seeking a responsible individual who values time management.*

Often supervisors are focused primarily on the skills necessary to complete the tasks in the job description. Consequently, they might forget about the skills needed for personal interactions with other team members and colleagues. Personal and professional development skills are just as important as job performance skills.

I once saw a job advertisement where the boss wanted someone who did not hum songs while working. You might consider that to be petty, in a job advertisement, but guess what!?! It was a small office, where coworkers with headsets answered phones near each other. Clearly, a chronic hummer had that position in the past and no longer filled it; that office environment was not a great fit for them. To each their own!

Your expectations should be worded properly in a job advertisement but be careful about anything inappropriate or illegal such as

> *Personal and professional development skills are just as important as job performance skills.*

discriminating against race, religion or sexual identity. Focus on specific qualities you are looking for. What are your expectations as a leader? Are there strengths you want your leaders to possess? Are you looking for coachable, respectful and proactive leaders?

Make a list of the qualities important to you, and keep it close by during the advertisement creation, interview process, and onboarding training.

After you've created the advertisement to attract your ideal team member and have at least a few applicants to choose from, it's time for my favorite part. Internet search! I love to search for people. Try adding quotations around a person's name when you do the search. For example: "Tina Levene" will focus the search on the entire name, anywhere it is found in the online world.

If you want to know about someone, search for them on the internet! You will find options to read, images (or mugshots) to look at, videos to watch, and social media pages. There are also a variety of public information searches you can do, free of charge. It will only cost you time. In the long run, you want someone who will represent you and your company well.

Even though I am a firm believer in second chances and recreating oneself, some past mistakes or behaviors are firm indications of future circumstances.

Before you start research on the new job applicants, decide what type of person you want on your team. Which extracurricular activities might make them ideal leaders? What strengths are you looking for?

We do live in an age where our personal lives reflect on our professional lives, like it or not. I can think of numerous, outrageous stories that were driven by the national media. The journalists did their homework and the truth was revealed in public court documents, in photos and on social media sites.

Once you have researched your candidates and their internet presence is acceptable for representing your company, then you are ready to strategize for the interview. Throw away those standard interview questions!

If you are looking for a positive, early riser who will be punctual, then schedule the interview for 8:00 AM sharp on Monday morning. Why at 8:00 AM? You will gain great insight to their attitude and punctuality by scheduling an interview first thing in the morning.

Why on Monday? Most functional users and abusers of alcohol or drugs will be partaking of their chemical substances on the weekend. With treatment costing companies more time and money than ever, an early Monday morning interview can give you some insight to their weekend activities. Before you judge me for that suggestion, let me share something with you.

I was one of those users and abusers of alcohol and drugs, as an employee. It takes one to know one I guess. Now, with over 20 years sober and clean, my individual experiences and my educational expertise makes me keenly aware.

To be honest, as much as I considered myself a functional employee at the time, being half-tanked is not a responsible way to show up for a job to take care of children! Intoxication is a serious safety issue for any job, particularly when operating machinery or managing other people's lives.

You can learn a LOT about a potential employee through the interview process. If you are looking for a flexible person that can go with the flow, call the candidate and reschedule the interview to see how they react. You will hear their attitude in their voice! When they arrive for the interview, thank them for their flexibility and watch for body language when they respond.

Another great interview strategy is to present a crisis during the interview. You can put your acting skills to work here. Ask your assistant to interrupt the interview with the crisis. Be sure it is believable and a problem that you have dealt with or could occur. As you react to the invented crisis, you can discover how the interviewee might respond.

Use the opportunity to ask how they might react in a similar situation. Be sure to ask open ended questions and allow them to identify solutions. While this is not a real-life experience, it will give you a glimpse of how you might work together as a team, and how the potential team member communicates and resolves conflict. This is all valuable information about what qualities they would bring to the position.

After you have selected the perfect team member, offered them the position, and they have accepted their new role, be sure to include a probationary period once employment begins. This provides a window of opportunity for you AND the new team member to determine if the position is a good fit.

Communication is the key to successful work relationships, but a performance review at the end of the probationary period gives the option for either party to walk away, and saves the company time, money, and energy. This is a proactive way to build a solid foundation for your team.

Another very important part of building a leadership team is the development of professional relationships. When you take a proactive approach to the job description, interview process, and the onboarding of your new employee, you will set an expectation for what is appropriate, acceptable and allowed in the organization. This is just the beginning of the process; you will continue to nurture professional relationships as you build your team.

Be aware, your team is always watching how you act and react to situations.

It is time to get R.E.A.L.

When you are proactive and creative while developing the job descriptions, implement constructive strategies in the interview process, and encourage open communication from the start with each new team member, you build a strong foundation for your team.

When you keep your values in the forefront of your mind, share your vision with the team, and encourage each team member to contribute their skills, you

> *Be aware, your team is always watching how you act and react to situations.*

become the cornerstone that takes on the weight of what you are building together while other's leadership abilities are being developed.

Amazing leaders are created, not born. You now have the tools to create a team of leaders.

Try these Action Steps:

If you have a position that needs to be filled in your company (or one coming up soon), use this for these exercises. If you do not, then choose a current position in your company and pretend like you need to fill it with a new employee and work your way through the steps below:

- Create a list of descriptions for that position.

- List out the non-negotiables – both the MUST HAVES and the MUST NOTS.

- Write an advertisement for that position.

- DO an internet search on a current candidate for the position or the person already in that position.

- Create a scenario you can use (see the example in the chapter) to test a candidate's or current employee's reaction and ideas.

- If a new employee is coming in, write down what you are going to look for during the probationary period.

"Go forth and perspire...or prosper!
Whatever you do, just keep being
awesome and developing!"

— Tina Levene

TINA LEVENE

Chapter Seven

Functioning as a Leader

"I never thought in terms of being a leader. I thought very simply in terms of helping people."

- *John Hume*

TINA LEVENE

Chapter Seven

Every leader desires to influence, impact, and inspire their team for legendary results. When a leader knows how to function with the heartbeat of a R.E.A.L. leader, they establish, develop, and represent leadership, in a manner that guarantees a profound greatness arises in every team member.

Authenticity in leadership creates harmony and builds emotional bonds between team members. It starts with self-awareness. Take an inventory of your own strengths, and identify your values, purpose, and core beliefs, so you can master and lead yourself first! Then you are ready to authentically lead others.

Your personal and professional development must work together if you are to be an influential leader. Another way to think of influence is *the sharing of your personal vision through your actions*, or a powerful articulation without words.

> **Every leader desires to influence, impact, and inspire their team for legendary results.**

Positive influence can be achieved when leaders recognize and manage emotions, this is often called emotional intelligence. Leaders use their emotional intelligence to influence their teams by recognizing AND connecting with them on an emotional level.

Your influence as a leader can affect the behaviors of your team both positively and negatively. If you are not able to control your own disruptive impulses or moods, you will see the results in their behaviors! If you are passionate and engaged, you will influence your team, community, and colleagues to be passionate and committed to the mission.

As a leader you will impact those that you manage, through the power of your influence. Team members will look to you for guidance and will modify their behaviors based on the relationships you create with them.

Your own emotional awareness and ability to communicate your vision will lay the foundation needed to impact your team and develop high performing leaders.

Leaders also impact their community beyond the work place. When you network with leaders from other companies, businesses, and agencies, you foster relationships and become the face of the company.

Your impact can lead to collaboration or partnership with other leaders BUT more importantly, the positive dialogue and constructive feedback will keep you coachable and evolving as a leader.

Let us talk about ants. Yes, ants! If you didn't know better, the communication and cooperation of ants could seem supernatural. It might look like ant telepathy, but in truth, ants use a chemical to alert each other to potential hazards or the promise of food. For example, an ant might find a huge piece of a sandwich someone carelessly dropped while walking in the park.

Even though a single ant can carry many times its body weight, this morsel might require a team effort to get it back to the colony

> *Your challenge is to build trust and be approachable, and you will inspire them to achieve more than they ever thought possible.*

where everyone can benefit. The ant sends out the chemical alert that food has been found and help is required to get the tasty treat home. That one find might nourish the colony for days or even weeks; talk about impact.

Another cool superpower of the ant is their stomachs. Yes, I said stomachs… as in two of them. Ants have two stomachs, not because they hoard food or need them for digestion. One stomach is for their own food and the other is for sharing with another ant, if the need presents itself. They take care of each other. What a great lesson for us as leaders.

What does it look like when we take care of our team? It could be a special snack in the breakroom occasionally or showing staff appreciation with an Employee of the Month program that includes a group celebration. Simple unexpected moments that honor team members will make them feel valued, and team members that feel valued are more engaged.

Managing people is not for the faint of heart. Creating a team that is effective and impactful can be overwhelming, complicated, and frustrating, at times. Each of them has unique personalities, gifts, and challenges. Your challenge is to build trust and be approachable, and you will inspire them to achieve more than they ever thought possible.

A R.E.A.L. leader will mentor and equip a team that is inspired to one day train others to lead as well. Balance positive and constructive feedback. Support other's growth and successes. Communication is key!

> *By working together, the team will connect the dots for the desired outcome, and you will have created a high-performance culture in the company.*

Remind your team often that you are ALL on the same team, you have the same mission, and you share the same vision. This is done very effectively in the military. Each individual soldier has a job to perform but they work together knowing they are all part of the same mission.

Think of a connect the dots game. You know the one where there is a hidden picture amongst the dots, but you don't see the picture clearly until you connect the dots in the correct order. Leaders are dot connectors! Think of each dot as a task, deliverable, or goal for your team. Under the guidance of the leader, the team works together to create the picture.

As a leader it is your job to communicate what the final picture should look like. Then you can translate that vision into smaller, meaningful goals for each team member to accomplish individually. By working together, the team will connect the dots for the desired outcome, and you will have created a high-performance culture in the company.

To foster sustainable achievement for your team and maintain a high-performance culture, you must start with the end in mind. Be sure your team is clear about your direction and then; dot to dot, task to task, and goal to goal, move your team (sometimes using baby steps) toward the ultimate mission.

Finally, you want to inspire your team to greatness. You can orchestrate unity or division in your team; the choice is yours. A R.E.A.L. leader understands there is strength in unity. A team that feels safe, celebrated, and valued will be inspired to perform at a higher level, accomplishing the team goals together.

It is time to get R.E.A.L.

Revolutionary leaders Elevate their teams and Activate their talents for Legendary results. My goal for this book is that it would teach you to guide and train your team, so they too can become R.E.A.L. leaders. This happens when you discover your strengths while celebrating other's gifts.

When you are functioning effectively in the role of a leader you are empowered to:

- Establish leadership (Influence)
- Develop leadership (Impact)
- Represent leadership (Inspire)

I believe that the only power you should have as a leader is to EMPOWER your team members. As you provide guidance and mentoring to your team, it will develop the skills needed to help them become great leaders. Actions do speak louder than words, and when it comes to leadership skills, they are often seen before they are heard. When team members see that you are coachable, they will be influenced by your example. You will impact your team every time you recognize a member for their skills and give credit where credit is due. A safe and nurturing environment will inspire your team to be engaged and high performing. May you influence your team, impact the world, and inspire those around you!

Try these Action Steps:

- Take an EQ Appraisal test and review the results.

- Assess what you can work on based on those results and put a plan in place.

- Ask your co-workers for feedback also to get ideas of how they see your EQ abilities because often people see us differently than we see ourselves. You want to know what actions are establishing you as a Leader and which ones may be hindering you as a Leader.

- Have your team members go through the same test and analysis so they can improve in this area also.

- Identify and implement ideas to take care of your team on an ongoing basis.

"The only time you should look down on someone, other than when you are lucky enough to be taller than me, is when you are reaching down to lift them up and empower them to be the best they can be!"

- Tina Levene

Chapter Eight

Communicating as a Leader

*"To effectively communicate, we must
realize that we are all different in the way
we perceive the world and use this
understanding as a guide to our
communication with others."*

- *Tony Robbins*

TINA LEVENE

Chapter Eight

What comes to mind when you hear the word communication? Do you automatically think about the words that slide out of people's mouths? Do you think of the actual verbiage that some spew out just to hear themselves talk? What if I told you that we can communicate without words? Would you believe me?

In this chapter, we will discover how *communicating as a leader* is relevant to your position. We will continue this journey of acknowledging your strengths, gifts, and challenges, as well as how to communicate a vision to your team. Not everyone on your team will communicate in the same way.

There are really three types of communicators out there in this world:

- Visual

- Auditory

- Kinesthetic

You may recognize these as learning styles. Communication styles, like learning styles, are vastly different from person to person. When we work to understand each other's communication styles, we learn to communicate effectively as a leader.

As you can envision, no pun intended, visual communicators watch what you say. They will watch your actions. They will read your words. They want written signs, everywhere. These are usually the people at work who make those rhyming signs for the bathroom, about cleaning up after yourself. There is usually a cute picture on the sign too. Do you work with these people? Visual communicators will often respond to a phone conversation with a follow up email, confirming what they heard in your conversation. Every team needs visual communicators.

Auditory communicators love to talk, talk, and talk some more. Did I mention they love to talk? These team members are the ones who will respond back to your text or email by calling you on the phone. They want to hear your voice.

Auditory communicators want to know that they are heard. They need confirmation that someone is always listening. They will ask if you understand what they are communicating, if you need clarification, and if they don't think you are listening, they will repeat themselves over, and over, and over again. Did I mention they'll repeat themselves? Every team needs auditory communicators.

Kinesthetic communicators are the people who need to pace back and forth while brainstorming. They tap their fingers or pen on the table top during meetings. Their feet are usually moving non-stop under the conference table. These are the team members that want to take notes, draw pictures on their notes, and enjoy videos and/or sound bites in colorful webinars.

You might want to tie them to their chair, but they are usually high energy, creative types that bring valuable 'out of the box' thinking. They strategize brilliantly and make for interesting conversations. Every team needs kinesthetic communicators.

As a leader, understanding your team member's way of communicating is very important. You want your team to understand your vision, but they will understand it in different ways. Some may understand when you communicate it verbally, while others might need an interactive presentation that includes colorful slides, music and a video. Each member of your team will communicate in their special way.

Team up with people who communicate differently than you do. By complementing one another's gifts, everyone feels valuable and will contribute. As a team, we need one another and our unique ways to communicate effectively.

When we educate our team, we use our communications skills. When you share strategies to manage time effectively, be mindful of the different styles in the group. If you create a communication activity at each staff meeting or conduct a ceremony of appreciation at the end of each month, understanding HOW your team members respond will help you create engagement. In other words, use everyday activities to teach leadership skills to your team members.

I once worked for an agency and we wanted to rebrand our reputation in the community. Instead of having a conference call or emails being blasted back and forth, our leader held a creative story boarding session.

It was very successful; each team member communicated in their own unique way. Some wrote stories, others drew pictures on the white board and others paced back and forth strategizing ways to drive home the new branding message to community partners. The leader facilitated the experience and allowed each person to communicate in their own way. The whole team learned how to strategically rebrand the organization; what a great opportunity!

Have you noticed how popular open-kitchen-concept restaurants have become recently? All the ingredients are separated in a clean showcase; you just pick what you want and create your

> *People want to know that a leader is credible and trustworthy before they are willing to buy into their vision.*

meal. This *create your own meal* concept is an enormous success. People like to have options, it gives them a sense of control. People also like to see the end result.

What if we as leaders could utilize this concept in our companies, agencies, and businesses? We could communicate our vision and then allow our team members to participate in the fulfillment of the mission in ways that create engagement and make them feel valued.

Imagine walking into a new doctor's office and not seeing their degrees or licenses on the wall. Would you wonder about their credibility? *Are they professionally educated and trained to treat me?* You may have a few questions in your head about the individual.

This could be why many CEO's have a big desk, in a big office, and display their prestigious college degrees on the wall in fancy frames for all to see. People want to know that a leader is credible and trustworthy before they are willing to buy into their vision.

Your team members also want to feel like they have a voice and are being heard. Active listening skills are essential in the role of leadership. There are a variety of ways to confirm that you are listening to your team; I use open ended questions to encourage open communication.

For example, ask a person how they are doing today. A personal response is required. People feel special when you show genuine interest in them personally. Once they respond to your open-ended question, use reflecting to respond back.

Reflecting is just that, reflect what they said to you. If they said they were feeling sick today, you could respond to them with "You are feeling sick today?" It confirms what the person said to you was heard when you reflect it back. You can also reflect with the summarizing technique.

Summarizing means you are listening to their response and summarizing it in your own words. A summarization of the above conversation may sound like this, "Oh no, I am sorry you are not feeling well today!" Summarizing is listening to the speaker's words and then repeating back to them as an indication that you understand what they are saying; it's a form of clarifying what you have heard.

Summarizing is a great tool to utilize in closing of staff meetings. I use it at the end of my meetings to clarify that I heard my leaders. I want them to know that their voice matters. Team members want to feel valued in their current job. Some ways a leader can communicate that team members are valuable to their company are acknowledgement, affirmation, and appreciation.

Acknowledging the concerns, questions or comments of team members adds value to their voice. Most people want to feel like their voice has been heard; others, just like to hear their own voices. When you acknowledge team members, affirm their presence is appreciated, their contribution is important, and they are valuable to the team.

Affirmations verify their worth to the team. Affirm that they are doing a great job. For some you might need to be more specific, "Your time management this morning for that meeting was impressive!" People want to hear what they are doing well. When team members feel their actions, words, and skills are affirmed, they will keep doing fantastic work! Keep positively affirming your team members and show your appreciation, each and every day.

Appreciation is a great way for a leader to celebrate their team. There are many ways to show you appreciate people. I highly recommend you find out what their love language is from the book, *The 5 Love Languages,* by Gary Chapman. Is it acts of service, quality time, gifts, physical touch or words of affirmation? Who doesn't like to be celebrated?

> *People want to hear what they are doing well. When team members feel their actions, words, and skills are affirmed, they will keep doing fantastic work!*

As a leader, celebrate your team by offering employee of the month awards, newsletters with a special spotlight section to highlight a team member's magnificent work, or Employee Appreciation Day when your team can wear jeans or get a free lunch.

There are many ways to show appreciation to your team, and it doesn't have to be a specific day or event. Every day you can show appreciation to one another. Just a simple, "Thank you for all you do," comment or a handwritten note stating *You are amazing! Thanks for being you!*

It is time to get R.E.A.L.

We learned a lot about communication in this chapter; it's so much more than just the words we say. Communication is what we do, and what we don't do. We communicate with our tone of voice, facial expressions, and body language. Our team members are always listening to what we do.

When leaders teach their team to lead and understand one another, the positive attributes, specific skills, unique gifts, and communication style of each member are acknowledged, affirmed, and appreciated. Celebrate those who share your mission today!

Try these Action Steps:

- Determine how each member on your team communicates best.

- Find out each team members 2 main love languages.

- How will you now interact with each person differently based on those 2 criteria?

GROUP SESSION IDEA:

Have each person take out a pen and paper and write down their preferred method of communication and their 2 love languages.

Have them fold up the paper and put them in a container and pass it around the room with each person randomly taking one out and holding on to it.

Once everyone has one, have them open it and be sure they didn't choose their own (If they did, have them swap with another person who chose their own). Then go around the table/room and have each person read the info off the paper they have.

This will keep people more interested and engaged and help them to get to know their fellow team members better. When done, collect them and have someone type them up in a Word document and send out to everyone on the team. They can refer to the document and get to know their fellow team members accordingly.

This can be a Powerful way to change your office environment for the better.

"You can attract more bees with honey,
but you should see the employees run for
the breakroom when you offer FREE
donuts!"

- Tina Levene

Chapter Nine

Celebrating Your Team

"It is better to lead from behind and to put others in front, especially when you celebrate victory when nice things occur. You take the front line when there is danger. Then people will appreciate your leadership."

- *Nelson Mandela*

TINA LEVENE

Chapter Nine

I'm sure we can all agree that people need to know they are appreciated! But imagine a workplace where team members are acknowledged and celebrated... one of the obstacles to celebration is comparison.

Let's talk about comparison... by now you are probably aware that I place high value on communication, let's be honest, as leaders it is key to our team's success. The voice of a leader can magnify differences or celebrate individuals for their unique skillsets. Again, it is your choice.

In my decades of work in professional environments, both government and non-governmental, my observation is that a leader either creates a language of comparison or of celebration with their team. It's important to understand the language of comparison, how it starts, and why it can be damaging to a team.

If you have siblings, you probably already understand the language of comparison. It starts when your sibling receives their first report card and your parents ask to see yours, too. It doesn't matter what grade level you are in, there is an unhealthy comparison going on between the two report cards and the siblings as individuals.

The moment you start to compete in sports and your parents attend the games and the banquets and begin to compare your sibling's trophy and accomplishments with your lousy participation ribbon. Whenever your performance and differences are pointed out in a less than flattering light, the negative comparison outweighs any possibility of "constructive criticism."

Even in relationships, parents tend to compare their adult children's successes. Who has been married the longest? Who makes the most money? Who has a house or who has the most *successful* career? Of course, the truth is, success is a subjective term, measured by whatever it is you personally value and consider as success.

With social media, comparison has become a dangerous scoring card to the personal perspective of the individual conducting the comparison with their own life. One thing I have learned in social work is that you never know what is happening behind closed doors.

I will never forget conducting a home visit at a huge, half a million-dollar home owned by a highly respected community advocate and executive. My client was his minor daughter who was abusing alcohol and drugs, merely a symptom of the trauma she was undergoing. After many assessments, investigations and therapeutic sessions, it was discovered to be one of the worst sexual molestation cases I have ever encountered as a social worker. And yes, it was her father who perpetrated it all.

For many years, I have helped women who struggle with addictions. One young lady that I worked with was extremely wealthy, but she struggled horribly with addictions. At the time, I compared my sober and clean life to her posh life. As a social worker, I was barely satisfying my family's basic necessities, and we lived pay check to pay check. She drove brand new luxury vehicles and lived in huge homes, and she didn't have to work even one hour for it. I was under the impression *she had it all*. After an inside look at her life, her addictions and mental health, I came to the realization I was extremely rich. I wouldn't trade the love, peace, joy and forgiveness I enjoy in my life for all the luxuries the world has to offer.

Comparison is rarely healthy, and it can be very damaging for a team. It creates a negative pity party for the individual. *Poor me, look at what they have, look at where they are going on vacation, look at what they are driving, I will never have that.* A pity party only allows reservations for "a party of one." Let's face it, no one else wants to be invited, and they certainly don't want to attend.

When we compare ourselves to other team members, we devalue who we are and damage our self-esteem. Sadly, there are others who are willing to do that for you, why bring that judgement on yourself?

> *Celebration language is positive and proactive appreciation of the gifts of your team members.*

Comparing your life to another's is like wearing blinders. You only see what is in front of you, not to the sides, or behind closed doors. Rest assured, there is always something going on that you and the public do not see.

The bottom line is, comparison language needs to be eliminated from your vocabulary, your home, and your work environment.

Celebration language is positive and proactive appreciation of the gifts of your team members. Celebrating others creates a safe and healthy environment. By thinking positively and having joy, your health improves from the inside out. Positive thinking, being optimistic and having an attitude of gratitude transforms your life and relationships not only in your place of employment, but in every area of your life.

You will attract likeminded people and those "Negative Nellies and Grumpy Freds" will drift away as they become uncomfortable with your positive attitude. What a great benefit! Celebration language is seeing others in the light of WHO they are and WHAT they have to offer; not just as an employee.

It reminds me of a time when I was growing up. I heard someone call my parents by their first names and realized they are real human beings with real lives. They were not just Mom and Dad, but people who had hopes, dreams, and aspirations of their own. They had successes, challenges and limitations, like all of us.

Great satisfaction comes from being truly happy for others when you celebrate with them. When a friend shares good news, removing your own wants or desires will help you stay focused on the positives in their life. It takes courage to put aside your own personal needs and celebrate the accomplishments of others.

Developing a professional relationship that recognizes and appreciates one another's accomplishments is the furthest thing from comparison language and gives every team member a great sense of satisfaction. It sets up a safe work environment that honors each other's gifts and accomplishments.

Celebration language can start in your staff meetings. Instead of setting up the staff meeting in the same ole' conference room, with the cold metal chairs and wood table dividing up the staff, try something different.

Purchase some casual furniture (perhaps bean bag chairs), a colorful light fixture and set up a microphone in the middle of the room. When your staff arrive, explain that you want to celebrate their gifts, not just what they bring to their professional life. Give them permission to use the microphone to sing, perform spoken word, rap, or comedy. Maybe have a white board for writing or drawing on and include a guitar or other instruments in case someone wants to share their musical abilities with the team.

Do NOT put pressure on your team to participate, anxiety is not the objective here! You will be surprised at the entertainment that is created by the gifts of your staff. Continue these comfy, celebratory staff meetings once a month. If no one runs up to the microphone to perform, just be silent. Silence is a motivator. You will see respect building, team building, and celebrations of one another's gifts almost immediately. These staff meetings will quickly become popular and an event the team looks forward to once a month.

There are many ways to celebrate other's achievements. It can be as simple as a greeting card, social media post, gift, phone call or text. When you develop an environment that fosters positivity, others are motivated to be more positive, and accomplish more, as well.

> *Revolutionary leaders will utilize the gift of celebration language to elevate their teams.*

It is magical when celebration language is spoken by a leader of a company, agency or business. It creates an atmosphere of hope and happiness that nurtures success. Your team will embrace the appreciation with open arms and an open heart. They will follow your example and start celebrating one another more and more. An added bonus, as their leader, you will be identified as a human being, not just a boss.

Sharing celebration language with your team will create a friendly rapport and continue to build professional relationships among your team. Team building will come naturally and more frequently. Every team member will flourish as they are celebrated. There is no better time than NOW to give up comparison language for the gift of celebration language.

It is time to get R.E.A.L.

Revolutionary leaders will utilize the gift of celebration language to elevate their teams. Gaining appreciation for one another is an authentic way to build team morale. Leaders demonstrate respect by building a team that not only respects one another but will identify and appreciate the uniqueness of each other's gifts in the work environment.

Before you say that this is all too warm and fuzzy, I want you to recognize that most people spend more time at their place of employment than in their own homes with their own families. So, for those thinking this is a bit much or it is too personal to talk about gifts and appreciation at work, try it!

Try showing others appreciation. Try transforming your language of comparison into celebration language. Bring awareness to other's gifts and uniqueness. Not only will you see a team that respects you, but you will build a fundamental relationship that encourages them to exceed their normal job duties.

Teams that feel valued and safe will perform to their best and highest abilities. Creating this higher performance culture produces more successful outcomes and sustainable staff that are healthy and happy. Happy team = team success! Celebrate your team today and every day!

Try these Action Steps:

- Identify any comparison language you catch yourself (or other team members using).

- Take that comparison language and find a more positive, celebratory way to express yourself.

- Make a list of ways you can show others appreciation and schedule a time to implement them.

> *"Like Kool and the Gang said, 'So bring*
> *your good times, and your laughter too.*
> *We gonna celebrate your party with*
> *YOU! Celebrate good times, come on!"*
> *Now that you are singing that song in*
> *your head, you are welcome.*
>
> *- Tina Levene*

TINA LEVENE

Chapter Ten

Building a Secure Team

"Be selective in your battles. Sometimes peace is better than being right."

- Unknown

TINA LEVENE

Chapter Ten

Have I mentioned the importance of a safe work environment for our teams? A clear vision, excellent communication, and celebration language are all great steps toward providing a sense of safety to team members. Healthy relationship building begins there, but there's more to building a secure team and it's a process that may not always be convenient or comfortable.

Let's chat for a bit about security, airport security. Flying to a faraway destination is very convenient nowadays. The airplane is one of the most innovative of inventions, if you ask me.

We pack a small piece of luggage or a couple of huge suitcases, depending on how many shoes you ladies pack! We travel to the airport, check in to receive our boarding passes while we hand over our suitcases to airline staff. We cross our fingers in the hope we will find our luggage at our destination. In the meantime, we head towards the gate to board our flight, but our journey is disrupted by a lengthy line of people waiting to be cleared by security.

When it is finally our turn, we juggle our carry-on luggage as we take off our shoes, belts and jackets. Next, we remove any laptops, keys and cell phones from our purses, backpacks and luggage. Now we stand in another line.

After all that, we walk through a huge x-ray looking machine. It not only detects bombs or dreadful things strapped to your body but is also a source of nervousness as you stand there, hands above your head hoping they cannot see that you have your ugly underwear or girdle on.

All the hassle of security makes you feel more stressed out than safe, doesn't it? The inconvenience of jumping through the required hoops is the high price we pay for added safety when we fly. It costs you some time, BUT your safety is priceless because you are priceless. A safe environment, a secure work place and an enriching employment experience is what every leader strives for at their company, agency or business.

I know, I know, you have heard me say it before. You can't ignore the importance of creating a safe environment for your employees. Just turn on the media and you will see that my paranoia is warranted by workplace shootings throughout the United States.

Security is important whether you work at the local fast food burger place or in a high rise in downtown New York City. Understanding your chances of danger and gaining knowledge about the consequences of not securing your workplace environment is always a dreaded task for a leader but it is a lifesaving task.

Am I implying that a metal detector and security guard should be assigned to every entrance of every business? No. Am I implying that employees can learn techniques to respect one another, become aware of red flags of aggression, understand the importance of letting go of pet peeves and develop a place of peace? Yes.

Leaders are the pilots of this journey where you choose peaceful relationships over being right. You can fly your team into troubled skies or prevent turbulence by completing your due diligence and adjusting your course when necessary.

One of my favorite personal mottoes for professional development is *Principles above Personalities*. Principles represent how we do the job or mission at hand and personalities represent well, the many personalities you must interact with day to day and week after week.

You are probably thinking, how do I work respectfully with a total jerk, someone that I have not even one ounce of respect for and thoroughly disagree with every personal choice this coworker makes outside of work? You need to be thinking, *what jobs or tasks are assigned to this employee?*

> *A culture of respect starts with you as the leader. You may not like someone personally, but you must respect them at work and work together on a team to the best of your ability.*

First and foremost, you need to detach; separate the professional coworker from the personal person. Remember, sometimes personal issues slither over to a person's professional life. In any case, being civil to every team member is important for your employees.

A culture of respect starts with you as the leader. You may not like someone personally, but you must respect them at work and work together on a team to the best of your ability. We can only control ourselves and our behaviors, in and outside of work. Leaders are prime influencers for interpersonal skill development.

Anyone is capable of learning a new skill set; in fact, most employees can afford to develop their interpersonal skills, to work more effectively with coworkers. Leadership is a balancing act of getting things done and having a genuine concern for people.

Employee conditions and morale matter just as much as productivity.

We understand that organization is a great vehicle for getting things done, and a team approach builds strong employee commitment levels. BUT, leaders that recognize and embrace a spirit of harmony and cooperation enjoy lower turnover rates and higher productivity. Additionally, group harmony gives everyone a sense of peace. Sign us up for that one, right!?!

Fighting battles daily can be exhausting and unnecessary. You will recall that Fire Fighters spend most of their time in training, being educated about preventing fires, rescuing people and being proactive about fire safety. As a leader, take time to educate yourself about prevention instead of just putting out fires.

A leader's responsibility is to encourage teamwork and motivate individuals without inquiring if they are worthy of it. Contrary to belief on social media, you are entitled to your own personal and professional opinion. Do you think every baseball player is best friends with their teammates? Do you think every hockey player loves their opponent? Of course not. Do athletes respect one another and work together no matter what? Yes!

Differences in opinions, ideas and personalities are natural when you work with a group of people. It is okay that your coworker has a different opinion than you do. You can still respect them and be civil enough to work together. R.E.A.L. leaders build team players. As a leader, you must disengage from the daily pressures, drama or distractions, and create a safe environment where employees can thrive, grow and live in peace with one another.

When necessary, utilize Employee Assistance Programs to resolve difficult issues. It is okay to remind your employees of these services. If your company does not offer these services, refer employees to outside help, support or counseling. Take time to develop trustworthy relationships with your team so you can have those heart to heart conversations.

As you strive for a peaceful work environment, you must pick your battles. Do you want to be right or do you want to have peace? If you said to be right, you may want to start over and read this book again!

As a leader YOU are the bridge between vision and community. The vision is the overall goal of the company. The community is the team working with you to accomplish the vision. The community shares the responsibility; however, the leader shoulders the responsibility of the outcome.

YOU have the responsibility to be self-aware and assess the impact of actions on situations. YOU must embrace self-discovery and be self-reflective as you develop into a R.E.A.L. leader. Your skills will grow as you learn, lead, communicate, solve problems, and resolve conflicts. Focus on your vision, passion, integrity, and humility.

Leaders listen! As a leader you will be called on to understand differences and overcome obstacles; keep an open mind and an open heart. Develop your ability to HEAR the opinions and ideas of your team members. Be aware that improvement comes through change, and sometimes changes comes with opposition and fear.

A great leader believes that resolution and change are possible and instills a sense of value and security in each team member. Every lesson is an opportunity for you to learn as a leader. Show your team that you are still coachable and willing to learn more.

Do you treat each person on your team as an individual? Do they feel secure and protected? Leaders create, develop and implement safety plans to

> *Be aware that improvement comes through change, and sometimes changes comes with opposition and fear.*

ensure safety, protection and security. R.E.A.L. leaders convey a positive attitude and work toward peace and harmony in the workplace. They assume responsibility for everything that happens in the company. Leaders who are willing to throw an employee under the proverbial bus or to hand off the mess for the team to clean up will quickly lose respect and credibility.

It is time to get R.E.A.L.

Revolutionary leaders Elevate their team and Activate their gifts for Legendary results. R.E.A.L. leaders create an environment where individuals willingly apply their unique gifts to a shared mission.

Leadership is about the relationship between leaders and their teams.

Try These Action Steps:

As a leader

- Be resourceful with your employees and seek solutions to any interpersonal issues they may experience. These issues may be occurring at home and you are just seeing the projection onto your employees.

- Support your employees by offering team building activities and staff appreciation events.

- Put in a plan to continually raise your awareness of the numerous outside conditions that may hinder your employees' performance at work (i.e. mental health, addiction, etc.) and then be proactive.

- Advocate for your employees.

- Activate their gifts and talents.

- Support their needs inside and outside of the workplace.

"You don't have to go bowling with your colleagues on a Saturday night, but you do have to respect them and work together as a team Monday through Friday!"

- *Tina Levene*

TINA LEVENE

Chapter Eleven

Developing Leadership Mindfulness

"Truly effective and inspiring leaders aren't actually driven to lead people; they are driven to serve them."

- Simon Sinek

TINA LEVENE

Chapter Eleven

For a leader, mindfulness is as important as breathing. Become an excellent model of self-care to your team. Establish balance in your personal and professional life. Cultivate awareness in each moment. Be conscious of issues. Solve problems proactively. Express gratitude. Maintain a positive attitude. And yes, stop and smell the proverbial roses. Don't have roses? Smell the coffee! Mindfulness requires that you breathe and breathe deeply.

I think we can all agree that staff bring their personal lives into their professional lives and vice versa. The number one factor in preventing burn-out is establishing balance of work and personal life. It is crucial to the process of sustaining self-care and wellness.

Encourage your team to take personal days, sick leave when ill, and vacation time, to spend time away from work. We are our best advocates for our own wellness. Only we can acknowledge when we need time to heal, need help or we are hurting. Time does not heal all wounds; however, it enables the space to start.

Mind over matter is a powerful tool to engage staff and create a positive workplace environment. Another activity I like to do with my Staff Development Trainings and Keynote audiences is entitled *Pain vs. Purpose.*

Pain vs. Purpose

I give each participant a rock. Yes, a real rock, about the size of a fifty-cent piece. I ask them to place the rock in their shoe, so they can feel it when they stand up and shift their weight around.

Then I ask them, "Does it hurt? Is it causing pain?"

Next, I offer a variety of candy options on a table and ask them to choose one. I ask them to place the candy in their mouth and savor the taste, as they walk to a new person in the room and introduce themselves.

After a few minutes, I ask them to end their conversations and return to their seats. Here are the questions I ask the participants after this activity:

- Raise your hand if you felt the rock in your shoe.

- Raise your hand if you could taste your piece of candy.

- Raise your hand if you had trouble listening to your new friend because you were focused on the pain in your shoe.

This simple activity draws their attention to three factors that may hinder or affect team building and respect of authority.

Pain, many people are in *pain*. It may be physical, emotional or spiritual pain. Each of us experience and exhibit pain differently. The difference among us is how we handle that pain. Some of us become short-tempered; others, quiet.

Some people hold onto it, focus only on the pain and allow it to control their thoughts, feelings and actions. Others of us may think, *it happened, it changed me, for the moment or a lifetime, time to move forward,* and let it go.

Each day, we somehow experience pain. It may be knocking our elbow on the doorway or a loved one's unexpected death. Pain can be a motivator to change or a justification of misery. The rock in the shoe represents pain in our lives and the choices we can make to handle it.

Pleasure, people find pleasure in a variety of things. The taste of good food or drinks, meeting new people, or traveling and new experiences.

Many of our pleasures stem from our passions. I love finding out what people are passionate about in their lives. If you are one of the lucky people, you are enjoying your passion each day at your place of employment.

Passion leads to pleasure, in and outside of the work environment. Maybe a good wholesome book gives you pleasure. One like this book? *wink wink* The piece of candy represents the pleasures in life and the choices we can make to enjoy them in the moment.

Purpose, why are we alive? Why were we created? What happens when we apply our gifts and talents to our passion?

When we are clear on our purposes, nothing can stop us. Not even pain can distract us from fulfilling our purposes.

After this activity I explain to the audiences that it is their choice. They can choose in any situation to focus their energy and time on pain or on pleasure. Pain represents a pause in their lives, while pleasure represents applying their passion to fulfill their purpose.

As a leader, it is your job to connect with your team and decipher to the best of your ability where each person is emotionally, physically, and spiritually. If all they are focused on is pain; you have a red flag indicating an underlying problem.

Being mindful of not just what is spoken by team members but what non-verbal body language is shouting even louder in the hallway and staff meetings.

Observe your team; watch what your team members are saying and doing. You may be amazed. Your silence will motivate your team to interact and allow you to detect underlying problems that might be hindering staff development, cohesiveness and team building.

Many CEO's, Business Owners, Executive Directors and Deans of Colleges or Universities contact me with a similar concern. They ask, "How do I engage my staff and create a positive workplace environment?" Their staff is challenging authority on a regular basis, and they show a lack of commitment and respect; change must occur.

After many years of investigating staff incident reports for government youth facilities that have become neglectful, abusive or abandoned responsibilities, I came to the same conclusion.

When a team member has one foot out the door, is stressed out or overwhelmed, they are a liability to the company. Bottom line - recognize the issue and resolve it quickly or pay the price.

Here are some of the signs I observe when engaging these individuals:

- Lack of eye contact
- Always placing blame on others
- No remorse for incidents they are responsible for
- Ungrateful attitude

As you work toward a resolution, start building a file now to document their sabotaging methods; better safe than sorry. They are like a ticking time bomb, ready to blow up at any minute.

Developing leadership mindfulness includes motivating your team, no matter how much you feel they are disengaged. A mindful leader uses awareness, acceptance and action, to bridge the gap between disengaged team members and themselves.

Learn to always nourish your team and keep them hungry for more. It is a proven fact; human beings are motivated by incentives, usually that includes pay checks or money to be exact. Think about it, we work to get paid and then we get paid, so we work.

Even for those not motivated by money, they still work to get paid, so they can afford a place to live, transportation, and food to survive. It is a vicious cycle of cat and mouse, around and around we go. So, why not make it a motivating and positive experience for your team?

People want to feel valued. I know, I know, you're thinking, *we discussed this already, Tina!* But it is a profound truth.

Think about when you go shopping. You don't just look at the price tags to determine which item you will buy, correct? You look at the function of the item. What value does it bring you and your life? Will it save you time? Will it save you money? Maybe it will help enhance your beauty or manliness? No matter the *why*, it is all about the value it brings you.

It is the same with people. They want to feel valued before anything else. You can empower your team by being an example, show them HOW to appreciate and value each other.

We have already discussed some great ways to demonstrate how much you value your team. You never know how a gift may make someone feel or the impact it will have on them. Feel free to think outside the box.

> *You can empower your team by being an example, show them HOW to appreciate and value each other.*

I had eleven surgeries in the last twelve years, three of which were life threatening. Just before my tenth surgery, I ran out of sick leave at my full-time governmental job. I will never forget how my team pulled together and donated eighty hours of their own personal sick leave to assist with my six-week recovery. It literally brought me to tears. What a blessing! Such a thoughtful and valuable gift at a time when I felt broken and helpless.

Another tool of the mindful leader is displaying gratitude every day; an attitude of gratitude.

> *Having an attitude of gratitude sets up a team for success.*

We all recognize that negativity, gossip and anger can be toxic in the work environment, however, gratitude can create a positive, healthy environment for a thriving team to succeed.

An attitude of gratitude sets the tone for team members to focus on their passion and purposes instead of their pain. I love the quote by Buzz Light Year in the *Toy Story* movie: "This isn't flying, this is falling with style."

Our attitude about everything in life, including our professions, lays the foundation for success in our personal lives and professional lives.

My dear friend, fellow work colleague and statewide leader, Andy Hindman displays an unstoppable and successful attitude in his book, *"This Is a Football."*

> *"I will work harder than you. I may be slow, but when I get there, you will know I had been there. I will do my best and play till the whistle blows."*

> \- *Andy Hindman, Author*

Attitudes can bridge the gap and build valuable relationships or drive a deeper wedge between enemies. Having an attitude of gratitude sets up a team for success.

Depending where you live in this world, take time to smell the leaves, summer morning dew on the grass or the freshly squeezed orange juice each morning. Find something you are grateful for.

Your attitude attracts your tribe; it's either positive or negative, it is your choice.

It is time to get R.E.A.L.

Leadership mindfulness is vital. It sets the foundation for developing a team of leaders. Show an attitude of gratitude to your employees through recognition award ceremonies, appreciation luncheons or encouraging time off. Solidify your trust and build valuable working relationships. Motivate one another to utilize your own strengths to prevent burn-out and support autonomy.

The ability to use mind over matter in circumstances that may cause stress or negativity, is a tool for effective leadership. Help your team to focus their efforts and passion on their purpose, and they will not waste time distracted by the pain in their lives.

You are now equipped with tools for mindfulness as a leader; take a moment, smell the coffee, and uplift yourself and your team!

Try These Action Steps:

- List out the specific things you can do as a Leader to recognize your team members and show your gratitude for them and schedule it, so it happens. Whatever "it" is do it weekly or monthly, on some regular interval and make "it" special.

- Schedule a time to speak to each team member and find out if they are in a pain or pleasure zone and if they feel they have a purpose. If they aren't in the pleasure/purpose zone, then work with them to find solutions to get them there. Do this at least 2 times a year.

- Find out what motivates each person and pair that with their love language to celebrate them in a way unique to them.

- On a regular basis, have your team members write out the things they are most grateful for.

"An attitude of gratitude not only helps you throughout the day, but you influence others too, especially those Negative Nellies and Grumpy Freds."

- *Tina Levene*

Chapter Twelve

Becoming a R.E.A.L. Leader!

"It's time to dig down deep to the core of who you are and find that inner strength and confidence that's been buried underneath the piles of debris and rubbish from your past failures and mistakes.

You have to roll up your sleeves and get ready to put in the hard work that's required, because as we know, nothing great comes without work."

- *Adonis Lenzy*

TINA LEVENE

Chapter Twelve

Congratulations! You made it! You are now equipped with the tools of a R.E.A.L. leader. For some of you, this might be the first leadership book you have ever read. For others, this will be added to your stack of leadership books, preferably on top, but I understand there are some big, famous names out there that deserve to be on top of the pile.

Leadership development opportunities come in all shapes, sizes, colors, and content. Maybe you never imagined being a leader before you read this book. Maybe you have never heard of me as an author. Maybe you've never heard me speak about creating high performance cultures. Perhaps the idea of leading people scares you or maybe you just wanted to read this book because you love the author so much. Please pick the latter of these. Thank you.

Whatever your motive was when you purchased this book, I hope it has exceeded all your expectations, and I really hope you learned a thing or two.

You are now equipped to lead the world! Okay, maybe not the WORLD, but your circle of influence – coworkers, family, or community organization.

What we do know is this, leadership is not just about your job title; it's so much more than a role or position.

> *Revolutionary leaders are made, not born.*

It's being a source of motivation for overworked and tired coworkers. It's being a voice of reason while negotiating a life-changing deal. It's encouraging your team when all they can focus on is a recent failure. *To lead* is an action verb; it's the cornerstone of a rock-solid foundation.

So, what IS a R.E.A.L. leader? **Revolutionary** leaders **Elevate** their team and **Activate** their talents for **Legendary** results... let's break that down.

Revolutionary leaders are *engaged in dramatic change.*

It may be a systemic change or a small personal change, a huge shift for your organization or a miniscule detail changed to impact a few. Whatever the change, a revolutionary leader will be engaged in the process from start to finish and will leave people and things better than before; a radically positive change.

Revolutionary leaders are made, not born. They are determined and persistent. A person may possess natural leadership abilities, but without determination and persistence, there will be no revolution. Revolutionary leaders are talented individuals with determination, dedication, and self-discipline, and a commitment to positive and lasting change.

Revolutionary leaders, *engaged in dramatic change,*

Elevate their team and *lift them to a higher position.*

Leaders elevate through trust, appreciation, and empowerment to create a safe environment where team members know they are valued. They use empathy to show the team they care about their well-being and not just their productivity.

When management focuses too much on productivity, a team will feel discouraged when projected numbers are not achieved. Everyone wants to feel heard as a human not just be a statistic that can be replaced. When leaders elevate their team, the focus is where it ought to be, on the value and humanity of each team member.

Revolutionary leaders, *engaged in dramatic change*,

Elevate their team, *lifting them to a higher position,* and

Activate their talents by *bringing dormant gifts into action*

Think about glow sticks. They can be pretty to look at, with a variety of shapes and colors to choose from, but their real value becomes evident when you activate them. Once you crack the inner tube and shake it up, a glow stick emanates a beautiful color, much brighter than the original stick you purchased. Essentially, a glow stick must be activated to fulfill its purpose. Likewise, a team that has been activated will shine brightly.

> *When leaders elevate their team, the focus is where it ought to be, on the value and humanity of each team member.*

If not activated, your team will be average at best. They will probably get through projects using basic skills without engaging their talents toward higher achievements.

Leaders who embrace the differences, encourage the development of unique skillsets, and celebrate the gifts of each team member activate their talents for results beyond the ordinary.

Revolutionary leaders, *engaged in dramatic change*,

Elevate their teams, *lifting them to a higher position,* and

Activate their talents, *bringing dormant gifts into action* for

Legendary results, *remarkable work creating lasting impact.*

Revolutionary leaders will run towards danger to keep others safe. The most selfless example, a hero of mine since we shared the same professional work experiences in social work, is the one and only Irena Sendler.

She worked for the Department of Social Welfare and Public Health of the city of Warsaw from 1935 to 1943. During this needless bloodshed of World War 2, this hero with her team of 24 others, rescued Jewish children by utilizing her leadership mindfulness, wisdom of social services, manipulative discernment, and protective intuitiveness.

She participated in their rescue, falsifying of legal documents for their placement into orphanages and other Polish families to save their lives from the holocaust. Her mission was to reunite them with their Parents. It is estimated she and her team saved 2,500 children from the fiery pits of the holocaust.

Even after being arrested in 1943 on the suspicion of these acts of heroism, before being brutally whisked off to prison where she was beaten and tortured, she never betrayed the children and protected the documents containing their falsifications, placements, etc. Her precious life was saved in the nick of time. Literally on her way to being executed by firing squad, her employer bribed the German officials for her release.

She continued working many years in the fields of nursing, social work and teaching. Often recognized as an inspiration and prime mover of the whole network that saved Jewish children, Irena has been decorated with numerous distinguished awards.

In many YouTube documentaries featuring Irena as the *Mother of the Jewish Children*, she states "As long as I live, as long as I have strength, I will profess the most important thing is goodness. Every child saved with my help is the justification of my existence on this Earth and not a title to glory."

I encourage you as a R.E.A.L. Leader to ask yourself every night these questions:

Did I do enough today?

Am I lifting others and celebrating their gifts?

Could I have done more to make this a better world?

The honest answers to these questions will serve as a guide as you implement a V.I.P. Standard (Value, Identity, Purpose) for working with every member of your team.

Value Standard - is about leaders who appreciate themselves and others, leaders who recognize that value is not found in credentials. Letters after a name may impress some, but if the person in front of those letters is not an asset to your team, they are of no value to the team.

A team member's value is more relevant than their financial worth to the company. Learn to recognize the value of your team members; they are priceless.

Identity Standard - is about leaders who cultivate self-awareness. Leaders respect a team member who has clarity about who they are, what they do, and how they do it. Team members who have established an authentic identity and are accountable to their own actions, have a sense of achievement.

Purpose Standard - is about leaders who encourage team members to use their passion to fulfill their purpose. Discovering strengths leads to connecting with their purpose which will help your team members experience fulfillment in their work.

Great leaders understand the need for humility and gratitude. Remember to be grateful for *the purpose* of each piece; their passion may have laid the foundation for your success.

It is time to get R.E.A.L.

Leadership comes with significant challenges, responsibilities and rewards. You will lead the charge for the company mission while guiding, mentoring, equipping and training others to become leaders as well. There could be some anger, gossip and negativity as you build your team, BUT you can be fearless knowing that the safe environment you foster will grow great leaders.

Hone your skills as a communicator; active listening and celebration language will assist you in connecting with your team members. As respectful relationships grow under your leadership, your team will thrive.

You may wonder what is next in your leadership journey; it is my hope that you have gained some insights and wisdom from these pages. Thank you for spending this time with me.

No matter how you viewed your leadership ability before reading this book, I believe YOU possess the potential to be a R.E.A.L. leader.

NOW is the time for your actions to speak louder than your words. What is your next step? Will you lead others on a mission? Will you train others to become R.E.A.L. leaders too? Perhaps you will become an unsung hero like Irene Sendler!

Whatever you choose to do now as a leader, do it with integrity, honesty and selflessness, BUT more than that be R.E.A.L.

I want to hear from you; connect with me on social media or get real with me at www.TinaTalksTruth.com and tell me about your next step!

TINA LEVENE

Resources

Quotes: John Quincy Adams, John Hume, Charles Lauer, Nelson Mandela, Diana Nyad, Tony Robbins, Eleanor Roosevelt, Irena Sendler, Any Stanley, Henry David Thoreau, Rick Warren, Zig Ziglar.

Chapman, Gary. (1995). "The Five Love Languages: How to express heartfelt commitment to your mate" Book, Northfield Publishing.

Hindman, Andy (2017). "This is a football" Book. XULON Press, 2017.

Lenzy, Adonis. (2015). "Next: what to do when you know there's something more" Book, Broadstreet Publishing, 2015.

Watson, Dr. Gretchen (2017, April). "Three Ways to Boost Workplace Safety" Psychology Today article

TINA LEVENE

About the Author

Tina Levene is a Professional Speaker, Trainer and Author who works with corporations, agencies, schools and churches to help them create a safe, positive, and high-performance culture.

As a humorous motivator and staff development trainer, Tina educates about leadership skills, igniting passion, preventing burn-out, and more.

Tina has excelled professionally, with over 20 years in both the corporate and the government sectors, focusing on the fields of Social Work, Drug Prevention, and Juvenile Justice.

Are you looking for a humorous motivational speaker who can deliver the solutions and outcomes YOU want for your audience in a FUN and memorable way?

Tina brings high energy, laughter, interaction, customization, and surprises around every turn with relevant content you can use to transform your work environment - all the elements you look for in a humorous motivational speaker!

Here are a few comments from conference coordinators world-wide who have booked Tina as their conference Keynote Speaker.

"Tina is a conference coordinators dream come true!"

"Tina is medicine for the soul!"

"Funny but REAL!"

"Both professional and personable. Tina's presentations mix laughter and learning all while rejuvenating souls!"

She absolutely loves being a motivating wife, nurturing mother, loving daughter, sister and friend to many.

When she is not on the stage, Tina loves writing, reading, fishing, and spending precious time with her son, family, and friends.

Made in the USA
Columbia, SC
11 May 2019